Sept.

To Joan — the word game player excepcionale!

Hours of fun to you

Cheers

Kurt Ostenn

WIT TWISTERS

by ARTHUR SWAN

Illustrated by
DOUG ANDERSON

Bell Publishing Company, New York

TABLE OF CONTENTS

About Wit Twisters

The first of these verses I attempted to solve was a rather obscure one my grandmother recalled from her younger days. She presented me with a short rhyme, generously sprinkled with blanks. After looking at the whole poem, she told me, I was to try to think of a four-letter word that would make sense in the first blank. If it was the right word, I could simply switch its four letters around, in various arrangements, and create four other words, each of which would fit sensibly into the remaining blanks. I puzzled over it for a whole day before giving up. Here is the verse she gave me:

> An _v_ _i_ _l_ _e_ old woman with _e_ _v_ _i_ _l_ intent
> Put on her _v_ _e_ _i_ _l_ and out she went.
> "Oh, _L_ _e_ _v_ _i_ she cried, "give me, I pray,
> "Some bread, that I may _l_ _i_ _v_ _e_ this day!"

Now that I am older and wiser, I realize that this was an unduly difficult poem on which to cut my Wit Twisting teeth. I also realize that the last blank of all is the easiest clue for many people to solve, since the final line suggests its meaning more clearly than do the others. It might be a good idea to work this anagram puzzle starting with blank number five.

Stop reading here, if you wish to puzzle this one through without help! For the rest of you, here is the solution. Blank number five is l-i-v-e. By rearranging those four letters, one arrives at four more words: evil, vile, veil, and Levi, which fit in that order in the first four spaces.

When I arranged this collection of Wit Twisters, it was my intention to place the easiest examples first. It proved impossible, however, to get any kind of agreement among the friends who tried them out; depending on subject matter, on mood, on word choice, or on luck, some people found one verse simple, while others claimed that it was obscure or impossible. My suggestion is that you leaf through this book and choose one that seems possible at first sight. After your first successes, plunge bravely into the rest, looking carefully in each case to see how many letters are required; some ask for three-letter words, some for six letters or more. Let the rhythm help you determine the number of syllables each blank must have.

Don't be too surprised if some Wit Twisters elude you for a day or longer. One or two may plague you throughout a cross-country trip. They are a time-tested remedy for car-sickness and airplane jitters. On the debit side, they have been cursed for keeping people awake long past midnight—so handle them with caution.

Good luck!

Arthur Swan

NATURE

ONE

Where man as yet no N E T S has spread,
In T E N S of hundreds, birds amass.
S E N T by the age-old call, they've sped
To N E S T in wild, familiar grass.

TWO

One of the A P E S escaped from the zoo!
It ran to the grocery. What a to-do!
It tossed P E A S and potatoes with zeal that was fiery
And was cornered at last in the A P S E of the Priory!

3

THREE

Quaint ⌐⊥∈⋈⊑ this hotel supplies
That don't appear upon the bill.
I speak of roaches, ⋈⊥⌐∈⊑, and flies.
You ⊑⋈⊥⌐∈ and slap; they're with you still!
At ⌐⊥⋈∈⊑ each guest ∈⋈⊥⌐⊑ pained screams
That ought to plague the owner's dreams.

FOUR

How patiently she ⊢◯∈⊑ the field
In hope of harvest's fuller yield!
One ⊑⊢◯∈ agape, her ⊢◯⊑∈ homespun,
She toils, serene, till work is done.

FIVE

The herd ⌐◯⋈⊑ gently on the homeward path.
With ⊑⌐◯⋈ but cheerful steps the farmboy strolls.
Above the piping choir of frogs at bath,
The quavering descant of the ◯⋈⌐⊑ unrolls. (?)

4

SIX

Marauding man, you _S H E A R_ the sheep
And hunt the gentle _H A R E S_ and deer!
No wood-god _H E A R S_ them, or in sleep
He'd make you _S H A R E_ your victims' fear.

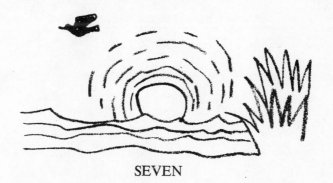

SEVEN

_L A T E_ is the hour, and still the lake.
Time, like a tedious _T A L E_, limps on.
At dawn, reeds glisten; birds awake;
A lone _T E A L_ rises, calls, is gone.

EIGHT

_S N U G_ in retreats still, leafy, deep,
The young _G N U S_ dream; quite safe they lie
From _G U N S_ whose lethal lullaby
Has _S U N G_ their mother fast asleep.

NINE

The L A M E hen clucks and limps around.
She spies some M E A L left on the ground.
The proud M A L E, dressed as for a fray,
Flaps up to snatch her crumb away.

TEN

Far from athletic T E A M S of apes,
And hidden from the lioness
Who tears M E A T S fresh from savage rapes,
In S T E A M and slime the pythoness
M A T E S with her spouse when passion boils,
And T A M E S his ardor in her coils.

ELEVEN

Tart juice of L I M E S the grinning lady sipped.
She'd walked for M I L E S to hear this rare crane's call.
From pools of S L I M E an alligator slipped
And ate that lady, L I M E S, fruit drink, and all.

TWELVE

"S C A T!" she cried, and C A S T a handy plate.
But still the C A T S behaved as their kind must,
Continuing (although the hour was late)
Their primal A C T S of jealousy and lust.

M

THIRTEEN

And now, each S E P A L of the blossom closes;
Each petal P A L E S before the sunset's roses.
But let the night L A P S E into brilliant morn,
Life L E A P S within: the flower is reborn!

7

FOURTEEN

Now does the sunset FOSTER calm.
On SOFTER breeze the muted bird-calls drift.
The insects of the darkening FOREST lift
Thin voices in an evening psalm.

FIFTEEN

The tiger LUGS the carcass to his lair,
Each panting breath a SLUG of fetid air,
While clots of blood and trailing GUTS betray
The way he came, and where surprised his prey.

SIXTEEN

You rustic Toms and KATES, give ear
To what is taught in Nature's schools.
STAKE all you have on country cheer;
Who search abroad for joy are fools!
Read KEATS or Blake by fruit-filled trees,
Or, when the ponds in winter freeze,

SKATE, laugh, and at the last, retire
To STEAK and beer by blazing fire.
The city's tables gleam and shine
With polished TEAKS and other fine
Imported woods. But country oak
TAKES wear, yet stands, like country folk.

SEVENTEEN

A tawny MANE and head emerged
Near priest and zoo-man disagreeing.
"How MEAN it is," the padre urged,
"To cage a great and wondrous being
"Born free to hunt in open air.
"In Holy Francis' NAME, forbear!"
"AMEN," roared deep the pious beast—
And munched that sympathetic priest.

EIGHTEEN

Streams LAVE the pastures which the warm sun kisses.
This grassy VALE the stranger's eye entices.
But herders waste no thought on rural blisses;
They dream of beef, of VEAL, and higher prices.

NINETEEN

The foolish – – – – – –, unaware,
– – – – – – much too far from water's edge,
Ignored the – – – – – – lurking there,
Was gobbled near the – – – – – – hedge.

TWENTY

The mouse's life with one – – – – – – closes.
– – – – – – pause upon their way.
On thorns among the roadside roses,
A – – – – – – impales its tiny prey.

LOVE GONE SOUR

ONE

Those blows were only _TAPS_ of love, he swore.
With friendly _PATS_ by chance he'd blacked her eyes.
Since in _PAST_ fights she had been pummeled more,
This _SPAT_ concluded with forgiving sighs.

TWO

If _TALES_ can be believed, my dear,
Time cannot _STALE_ your seasoned charms.
Yet I would give at _LEAST_ a year
Could I but _STEAL_ to younger arms!

13

⊚

THREE

She had been RAPED, she gasped, devoid of strength—
Then paused to DRAPE her gown across the booth.
The PADRE listened, questioned, and at length
PARED down her story to a simpler truth.

FOUR

The Devil looked within the – – – – – – and saw
A – – – – – – of lewdness hidden from our sights.
The cunning – – – – – – then played upon this flaw
With dreams of – – – – – – feminine delights.

FIVE

Their cries – – – – – – –. Do not your false hearts ache,
– – – – – – – of your loved ones' perfect trust?
Were there no – – – – – – – paths for you to take
Than these unhealthy ones of heartless lust?

SIX

The two great ⌐ＡＤＬＥＳ, proud and grave,
ＳＡＬＬＥＤ grandly down the darkened nave,
But in its ＡＩＳＬＥＤ recess bewept
ＬＤＥＡＬＳ lost while Virtue slept.

SEVEN

She ＳＡＮＧ of love ere they were wed,
And looked to him for reassurance.
Since then, a ＳＮＡＧ has raised its head:
She ＮＡＧＳ at him beyond endurance.

16

OUT OF MY WITS TWISTERS

ONE

Her lover's _PLEA_ sounds distant, dim,
Through thunder's _PEAL_ and swirling gloom.
Her _PALE_, crazed face stares o'er the brim
Till, with a _LEAP_, she seeks her doom.

TWO

The moon was but a _SLIVER_ thin;
No _SILVER_ light its spare arc gave.
The ghoul lured weary people in
And munched their _LIVERS_ in his cave.

THREE

Did no shriek _MAR_ the silent night,
When foes crept up to _RAM_ the gate?
The sleeping city woke too late
To _ARM_ against that savage might.

19

FOUR

An unseen $\leq \;\vdash \angle \;\top$ let water through.
The ship began to $\angle \perp \leq \top$ and sway.
That night, full soundly slept the crew
On beds of $\leq \perp \vdash \top$ and sucking clay.

FIVE

"Look! Native $\vdash \;\cup\; \top \leq$! How quaint!" she cried.
"They don't look $\leq\; \vdash \cup \top$. Let's go inside!"
Her husband's "$\top \cup \leq \vdash$" was overruled;
$\top \vdash \cup \leq$ they were cooked ere evening cooled.

SIX

"Don't $\subseteq \triangle \mathcal{I} \leq \mathcal{R}$," said the lady, "to the masses
"Or $\mathcal{R} \leq \triangle \subset \mathcal{I}$ to their opinion's churlish choice."
She was shoved into a $\subseteq \mathcal{B} \triangle \mathcal{I} \leq$ marked POISON GASES.
Strange! No $\mathcal{I} \mathcal{R} \triangle \subset \leq$ was found of her (or the invoice).

SEVEN

The girls began to *ILRE* before they gained
The topmost *ILER* hewed in that cliff of stone.
Throughout the *RILE* held fast, at last unchained,
Each maiden leapt, or to her death was thrown.

EIGHT

The *SLOOP* goes down. Her men are drowned
And sink to murky *POOLS* below.
By *LOOPS* of seaweed loosely bound,
They drift, pale corpses, to and fro.
Their lives, brief threads that raveled toward the light,
Are wound again around the *SPOOL* of night.

NINE

The _ _I_ _D_ _E_ _S_ dawns grey. The tyrant walks,
Ringed by false friends, and idly talks.
Blades pierce his _S_ _I_ _D_ _E_ and hack him down.
He _D_ _I_ _E_ _S_, wrapped in his blood-soaked gown.

TEN

The child stands awe-struck in the gloom.
That – – – –: is it of the tomb?
He sees the – – – –, where Jesus died.
He hears the – – – –: is shut inside!

ELEVEN

The sharp-horned moon – – – – – troops of swollen clouds
That spill their rain-blood on the corpse-strewn plain.
Of – – – – – and brambles, witches weave great shrouds
For – – – – – by the mightier Giants slain.

TWELVE

The drowned ship rocks upon its weedy bed.
A S P A S groans, shifting with the tide.
R A P S from within seem signals from the dead,
Till doors R A S P shut and lock the sound inside.

REPENTS

THIRTEEN

"Too late the witch – – – – – – –," the prelate cries,
As on his horse he – – – – – – – toward the square.
"In – – – – – – – she has learned the Devil's lies!
"And now she'll burn, despite her tardy prayer!"

FOURTEEN

By murky – – – – – – and boggy glen,
Near – – – – – – unknown to sailing men,
The – – – – – –   – – – – – – off their slime and steal
To churchyards for their loathsome meal.

FIFTEEN

Her potent – – – – – subdued the lusty crew.
Each manly arm, each – – – – – –, flaccid grew.
Dull lethargy, like mist, engulfed them all.
As brutish – – – – – –, they fled the witch's hall.

SIXTEEN

The patient – – – – – – – of that torn tome found,
In – – – – – – – once used at Borgia's balls,
The one – – – – – – – amount of glass, which ground
And mixed with sweets, best – – – – – – – stomach walls.

SEVENTEEN

The guards do still – – – – – – – thee, royal ghost,
As if thy – – – – – – – shone with stones more real
Than these of mist and moon; as if thy host
Of warriors could, poor – – – – – – –, breathe and feel!

EIGHTEEN

She could DISCERN no pity in his face,
Yet pled with the stern tyrant, throned above:
"Reduce this block to CINDERS! Show him grace!
"RESCIND the sentence! Spare the man I love!"

NINETEEN

Below the lowest – – – – – – of her mind
Some instinct stirs, – – – – – – its danger call,
And rouses her to search—and thus to find
The blood-crazed – – – – – – scrambling up her wall.

TWENTY

The lovers – – – – –, for murder is their aim,
Between great – – – – – that roar with hidden flame.
They seize her husband, thrust him toward the fire,
And forge new – – – – – of lust beside his pyre.

HOPES AND THOUGHTS

ONE

The *PEON* toils for rice and beans.
For *PONE* the simple plowmen sweat.
"Our daily bread"—how much it means!
With *OPEN* hand, Lord, feed us yet!

TWO

This paper chose to *EDIT* news
To serve the *DIET* readers sought.
TIED to that policy, its views
Changed with each *TIDE* in public thought.

THREE

He taught his – – – – – to sing, when he was young,
Of toil, of sweat, of those who – – – – – unsung.
No force could – – – – – him from labor's fight!
Yet, middle-aged, he – – – – – toward the Right.

FOUR

Our junk-heaps, – – – – – of metallic blight,
Are graveyards of things no one – – – – – for here.
Poor future – – – – –, seeking past delight!
We'll – – – – – you with this sordid souvenir!

PILES

FIVE

The – – – – – – – knots we ever tie
Are tangled – – – – – – – of fear or doubt,
Or – – – – – – – – that we twist and ply
Till understanding sorts them out.

SIX

Caught is the – – – – of white lies
By Satan's subtlest – – – – of all.
He is quite – – – – of Paradise
Until, too late, he – – – – his fall.

SEVEN

Past tumbled pillars and through – – – – – – dim
The – – – – – – still pursues, relentless, grim.
The objects of his – – – – – – no harbors find:
Death is the hunter, and His prey—mankind.

EIGHT

Alone, among high _PEAKS_, he prays:
"O God, Who _SPAKE_ in ancient days
"To Moses on the mountain's brow,
"_SPEAK_ to Thy waiting servant now!"

NINE

His life, grim search for – – – – –, ends
In luxury, but without friends.
An – – – – – plagues his final days:
Self-torture for his – – – – – ways.

TEN

– – – – – – with God, what cannot martyrs do?
Consider – – – – – –, or blind Samson's plight,
Or saints who, – – – – – – or burned or torn in two,
Brooked no – – – – – – of their Master's might.

ELEVEN

The peaceful – – – – blessed this fruitful plain.
Our – – – – were rich with ripe and rippling grain.
Full – – – – and golden sheaves we'd harvest still,
But war has come, and all is – – – – and chill.

32

TWELVE

This – – – – – marks the passing of each hour,
Unmindful of man's – – – – –, need, or power.
No holder of the – – – – –, crown, or mace
Can make one hour – – – – – its steady pace.

THIRTEEN

The _EASTERN_ sky gives promise of the day,
Gives _earnest_ of a life that has no end,
And makes the distant goal for which I pray
Seem close to me as is my _nearest_ friend.

FOURTEEN

Swift change – – – – – – when spring's soft rains
Bring – – – – – – to the thirsty plains
And, yearly, moist appointments keep
To rouse each – – – – – – from its sleep.

FIFTEEN

This fetid – – – – – of life is man's mistake.
O Nature, – – – – – our tawdry world anew!
From these unsightly – – – – – of refuse make
A garden spring, all bright with bloom and dew.

SIXTEEN

From War's old worship, – – – – us, God!
Let hatred – – – –, and bring to birth
– – – – upon this ravaged sod
An Eden-fresh and loving earth!

SEVENTEEN

The leaders turn A S I D E and whisper low.
Their A I D E S respond so humbly, yet we know
That the I D E A S which their masters spout
Were by these underlings first reasoned out.

EIGHTEEN

I once *RELIVED* in thought my past mistakes,
And oft *REVILED* myself with bitter force.
But the old Self itself through love remakes;
New thoughts *DELIVER* me from old remorse.

NINETEEN

Though he – – – – – – punishment by law,
His efforts to – – – – – – himself were vain.
The sentence of the Court was light, he saw,
While long he – – – – – – with remorse and pain.

TWENTY

Most gifted – – – – – – – of that muse-touched throng—
The – – – – – – – and the bards of ancient Troy—
Your artistry lent each time-hallowed song
Some – – – – – – – poignancy or keener joy.

FOOD AND DRINK

ONE

What made the dust-stained hiker smile?
What made him S L N G and jig awhile?
A S I G N it was, whose pictures showed
The ales and G L U S served down the road.

TWO

The old man B A R E D a yellow grin.
Dark yellow stained his B E A R D and chin.
Tobacco was his meat and drink;
He chewed it more than B R E A D, I think.

THREE

The old Dutch D A M E urged, "Have some more:
"More E D A M on my fresh-baked bread."
Her beer was sweet as M E A D of yore
(But M A D E in her bath-tub, 'twas said).

FOUR

The old cook _NAPS_ with head on shoulder.
Her dreams _SPAN_ all her dreary years.
The unwatched _PANS_ are growing colder,
Till with a _SNAP_ she wakes in tears.

FIVE

Don't blame the poor cowboy, who from the _WEST_ rides,
If with raw alcohol he _WETS_ his insides.
For the _STEW_ that he cooks to fill up his gizzard
Is a mixture of cactus and filet of lizard!

SIX

Poor ship-wrecked men, for sea-girt – – – – – – bound!
With – – – – – – looks they viewed this unknown ground
Where – – – – – –, halved, their pale, sweet flesh displayed,
And – – – – – – breathed cool fragrance from the shade.

SEVEN

By virtue of her skill with *MACE* and sage
And other spices new to that dark age,
Her cooking *CAME* to be revered, apart:
The *ACME* of the culinary art.

EIGHT

Great Cyclops chewed, like *NUTS*, the skulls of ox and horse,
And human flesh washed down with *TUNS* of wine.
His soft caress could *STUN*; yet this gigantic force
Was tricked by Thought and speared by sly Design.

NINE

She *TIPS* her basket, spilling cherries,
Toothsome pears and juicy berries.
The children, while demanding more,
SPLT cherry *PITS* upon the floor.

TEN

His empty *GUMS* the old man showed
In gaping, *SMUG*, derisive smile.
"Come, tapster! *MUGS* for all!" he crowed.
"We'll toast old age and gold awhile."

ELEVEN

He claims that – – – – – make – – – – – his hair,
And garlic's his complexion's care.
He looks the handsome, dashing rover,
But oh! his breath quite – – – – – one over.

TWELVE

Tonight he's – – – – – merry with the guys.
Tomorrow, he'll – – – – – to toss 'em back.
By Friday night, this – – – – – will win the prize.
All weekend, he'll stay home with the ice pack.

THIRTEEN

The – – – – is quite fat and tall,
But no one likes its stringy meat;
And though the – – – – is rather small,
I – – – – it's good to cook and eat.

FOURTEEN

The heads of great – – – – – – – arrive in town
To meet and fix the prices of their wares.
In costly – – – – – – – they attempt to drown
Their – – – – – – – guilts and leaden-colored cares.

FIFTEEN

The busboys now – – – – – – – the rented plates
And from the – – – – – – – lift the hired table.
The – – – – – – –, who such brief myths creates,
Must for some other host – – – – – – – the fable.

SEA, SKY, AND OPEN SPACES

ONE

Down the – – – – she slides and meets the sea,
Plunges, – – – –, and comes at last to ride
Serenely on the forceful, swelling tide
Beneath whose – – – – from this day she must be.

TWO

I found a – – – – – – gasping by the shore,
And though its – – – – – –, found I could no more
Its keeper than its wanton killer be—
And so returned old Neptune's – – – – – – to sea.

THREE

Three – – – – – burst on the shuttered bungalow
And peered between the – – – – – for deviltry.
The horror that they saw still – – – – –, although
They seek forgetfulness from sea to sea.

FOUR

For inspiration's sake this trip was made;
Yet when they sailed that – – – – – –, and seas were rough,
The – – – – – – moaned that he would gladly trade
His finer – – – – – – for some of stouter stuff.

FIVE

The flashing minnow – – – – – – in the rill.
Slim – – – – – – seek the vastness of the sea.
The tide, with lunar – – – – – –, lifts until
Your skiff drifts gently on the stream to me.

SIX

The – – – – moaned, "The climate here
"Is worse than in my desert town.
"When I went north, – – – – nipped my ear.
"On my way south, – – – – bogged me down!"

SEVEN

The – – – – – – island drowses in the sun.
Like – – – – – – on the hills, its silver streams
– – – – – – in reedy – – – – – –. Journeys done,
They – – – – – – to the sea that, sighing, dreams.

EIGHT

Enjoy these country hours, too brief.
Untie the ᴚ ᴐ ᴘ ᴇ ᔆ; row to the reef.
The city's ᴘ ᴚ ᴐ ᔆ ᴇ now put aside
For poetry of wave and tide.
With magnifying glass, behold
The smallest ᔆ ᴘ ᴐ ᴚ ᴇ and sprouting mold,
Or ᴘ ᴐ ᴚ ᴇ ᔆ that, in this slender leaf,
Seem craters deeper than belief.
Your snug, French "Mon ᴘ ᴇ ᴘ ᴐ ᔆ" is nice,
But out of doors is Paradise!

NINE

He *P A C E S* daily, to and fro,
The *S P A C E* within his narrow cell,
And dreams of seas, of *C A P E S*, of snow,
Of jungle heat—but wakes in Hell.

TEN

When she – – – – – – her quiet country place
To live amid the – – – – – – of the town,
She'd call to mind her – – – – – – aster's face
To help her fight the city's drabness down;
While paler – – – – – their dear magic lent
Until she thought she breathed their – – – – – – scent.

ELEVEN

The track – – – – – – west across the grassy plain.
Some grazing – – – – – race off as the train
Comes sighing in, each – – – – – and each wheel
Proclaiming its exhaustion with a squeal.

TWELVE

No fault or _S E A M_ disturbed the land's smooth crust;
The prairies rolled, the _S A M E_ on every side.
Abruptly then, the _M E S A_ skyward thrust
Its massive monument of granite pride.

THIRTEEN

Through seas of – – – – – they have flown—
These – – – – – explorers of far skies—
And – – – – – have seen things once unknown
By any save immortal eyes.

FOURTEEN

Like one of Queen Mab's _C A R S_, the airplane came,
High soaring even as its engines died.
In silver _A R C S_ it fell, to crash in flame
And etch that _S C A R_ along the mountain's side.

FIFTEEN

The ~~– – – –~~ and his belovéd lay on deck
And smiled at every S T A R that smiled on them,
Until three R A T S breathed down her lovely neck—
Whereat his lady flipped her diadem!
But he recalled the A R T S of chemistry,
Distilled some lethal T A R S, and killed all three.

SIXTEEN

The haddock thinks – – – – – – secure at sea
And scorns the fishing boat the ocean tosses;
And yet tomorrow, its – – – – – – will be
Sliced up to – – – – – – under heavy sauces.

SEVENTEEN

The stars A R I S E, in gleaming troops amass,
And R A I S E bright emblems blazoning their birth.
Now Pisces wheels, to let bold A I R E S pass,
And each in turn sheds blessings on the earth.

EIGHTEEN

The swimmers' bodies – – – – – – – in the sun,
Where salt air – – – – – – – like the surf, its twin.
The time for – – – – – – –, scarf, and cap is done,
As winter's wraps give pride of place to skin.

NINETEEN

She hears the stream that _RACES_ down the hill
And sings through wooded _ACRES_ its sweet psalm.
The _SCARE_ and turmoil of her life grow still
As city _CARES_ give way to country calm.

TWENTY

She _OWNS_ that gardening has kept her young—
That when what she has _SOWN_ has newly sprung,
And leaves uncurl in every garden bed,
The _SNOW_ of age lies lightly on her head.

PIETY AND POSE

ONE

That SOBER parson, mien so meek,
Whose ROBES are modest, and whose cheek
Invites us, "Slap me, sinful vermin,"
BORES us weekly with his sermon.

TWO

Before the – – – – –, long revered, he stands—
The – – – – – of a Russian house, once proud.
His last few – – – – – he lets slip through his hands.
Then on his knees he weeps and prays aloud.

THREE

– – – – – rustle by the altar rail.
Small – – – – – glow through a smoky veil.
A – – – – – curls through the scented air,
Calling folk to Easter prayer.

FOUR

The deacon — — — — — —. Their deeds extolled,
The — — — — — — sit there, looking humble.
Their rich — — — — — — is growing cold.
— — — — — — dwindle; stomachs grumble.

FIVE

To speed the — — — — — — — knight to war,
The priest his argument — — — — — — — — switches.
He pleads — — — — — — — — of God no more,
But plays upon the knight's desire for riches.

SIX

Cain was W R O T H, and his countenance fell,
For he knew the W O R T H of his offering well.
Why did the Lord T H R O W him looks of disdain,
While He made His acceptance of Abel's gifts plain?

58

SEVEN

The minister advised – – – – – – – youths
That they were – – – – – – – down to fiery coals:
"Cast off your doubts! Embrace God's truths!
"Oh, wash the sooty – – – – – – – from your souls!"

EIGHT

Such music Mozart left us when he died!
Was mortal man the – – – – – – of its line,
Or had some – – – – – – graciously supplied
Each deathless – – – – – – from harmonies divine?

NINE

Toward God her – – – – – – life must send out,
Like mild – – – – – –, a pious mist.
One hates to – – – – – – her fame with doubt,
But I have heard she – – – – – – at whist!

TEN

The leader of the – – – – – – stood where shade
Of ancient – – – – – hid his troubled face.
For his – – – – – –, tired men he prayed
That – – – – – – might would shield them from disgrace.

ELEVEN

The pastor, on the $\underline{D}\ L\ \underline{A}\ \underline{S}$, closed his prayer,
And sanctity and silence filled the air.
Those $\underline{A}\ \underline{I}\ \underline{D}\ \underline{S}$ to Kate's digestion failed again,
And loud and clear, her stomach $\underline{S}\ \underline{A}\ L\ \underline{D}$, "Amen."

TWELVE

The vast – – – – emptied; great bells pealed.
– – – – climbed the high church steeple,
Put the – – – – in place, then reeled,
And fell to death among his people.

THIRTEEN

No – – – – – was she, though much by men adored.
Her soul's dark – – – – – she prettily deplored,
While hiding it from sight behind bright gems
Or – – – – – gowns and dazzling diadems.

FOURTEEN

While lengthy sermons, – – – – –, may sound fine,
I'm – – – – – to recall one clear-cut line;
For like a – – – – –, which with time must wane,
The more you – – – – –, the lower ebbs my brain.

FIFTEEN

With – – – – on her lips, the abbess dies,
Where none can see – – – – thieves who struck her down.
The holy – – – –, the sought-for vessel, lies
Unseen and safe beneath her flowing gown.

POLITICS, PRIDE, AND PRICE

ONE

With long-forgotten tales, the wily sage
– – – – – savage tempers that were cool before,
And fans their ancient – – – – – to present rage
Until with – – – – – they arm and ride to war.

TWO

Unwise she was to BRAG about that gown,
And say her GARB would put the Queen's to scorn.
The Queen cried, "GRAB her! Lead her through the town
"Clad as she was by God when she was born!"

THREE

Behind toppled P L U E S, he knelt down in the mire
And waited to S N I P E at the foe as they fled.
He shot as they passed, but their answering fire
Shattered his S E L N E, and the rebel fell dead.

FOUR

The S L A V E kneels by the wounded, conquering chief
And L A V E S his cuts and soothes their aching pain
With S A L V E, but weeps within, "Restore me, thief,
"Unto my country's peaceful V A L E S again!"

FIVE

"Great Spartacus is S L A I N," they wept.
"The cruel N A I L S have torn his flesh."
Like some low S N A I L his people crept,
Who once had marched courageous, fresh.

SIX

To _SHORTEN_ reigns of kings who misuse might,
The entomologist can do his bit
By stealing to the monarchs' _THRONES_ at night
And hiding nests of _HORNETS_ where they sit.

SEVEN

The nation that _REVERES_ its king today,
Quite the _REVERSE_ tomorrow, ends his sway.
The Fates _RESERVE_ their wrath, but will invoke
SEVERER justice still upon his folk.

EIGHT

The _WARDER_ shoved the notice out of sight,
But pulled it from the _DRAWER_ to read that night,
And _WARRED_ within himself how best to spend
The large _REWARD_ for turning in his friend.

NINE

His – – – – – – sealed the doom of his young wife,
But mounting guilt now – – – – – – his whole life;
And the old king, for all his feasts and routs,
Must still – – – – – – the poison of his doubts.

TEN

The *NEWS* she'd shared with us convulsed the court:
She said that since she'd failed to pay those men
For taking off her *WENS* (and one large wart),
They wickedly had *SEWN* them back again!

ELEVEN

To magazines that serve up earthy mirth,
This raconteur – – – – – – – his tales risqué.
A – – – – – – –, he calculates their worth:
The – – – – – – – his tale, the more his pay.

TWELVE

Our older – – – – – – get on with their trade
And sell or mend the coverings they've made.
Their sons, however, – – – – – – precedent
With – – – – – – – and strikes and bitter argument.

THIRTEEN

The Philistines, like HARES, disperse in fright.
Alone, Delilah HEARS the frantic rout.
She scorns to SHARE their awe of Samson's might,
Of which she'll SHEAR him ere this night wears out.

FOURTEEN

The – – – – – – novice, casting flies at dawn,
Respects the – – – – – – where the large fish spawn;
But Commerce, that should value Nature more,
Too often is the – – – – – – of her store.

FIFTEEN

With _O V E R T_ and with subtle means, he woos
The uncommitted _V O T E R_ to his side.
The (_ _ _ _ _) he covets glints beneath the ooze
Of sullied conscience and placated pride.

VETOR
OVERT
VOTER
R V
E T O

SIXTEEN

What awkward _C R I T T E R S_ we poor mortals be!
From all that would _R E S T R I C T_ us, we'd be free;
Yet with the first of freedom's growing-pains,
We grow afraid and look for _S T R I C T E R_ reins!

SEVENTEEN

KNIFE

This rusted _S W O R D_ gleamed at some Saxon's side,
A burnished symbol blazoning his pride.
Yet Time conspired to _ _ _ _ _ _ it of its glow
And _ _ _ _ _ _ mankind how brief is earthly show.

EIGHTEEN

Tom first risked nickels in a ⊆⊦⊆⊏, to see
If luck would bless him more than industry.
He then risked ⊦⊆⊥⊆ and houses when he played,
And ⊦⊆⊆⊥ at last the fortune he had made.

NINETEEN

Our – – – – – men suggest the ways of peace.
Our standing army – – – – – itself for war,
To give the nation's – – – – – swift release
When Wisdom's voice is credited no more.

TWENTY

His fortune was *RELATED* to the sea
And *ALTERED* with each ship's success or wreck.
One day, *ALERTED* to catastrophe,
He staked his fortune on a drier deck,
Which he *REDEALT* and shuffled, till he struck
The *TREADLE* on the golden wheel of luck.

RELATED
ALTERED
REDEALT
ALERTED

72

PASTIMES, PEOPLE, AND PROFESSIONS

ONE

How could she _DARE_ to say she'd sing
The role of (_DARE_?) at the Met?
Why, notes don't daunt the _DEAR_ old thing:
She hasn't learned to _READ_ them yet.

TWO

Poor Lonesome Lenny played his – – – – where
Those two side streets – – – – upon the square.
But city laws have stilled the tuneful hermit,
Since concerts are – – – – without a permit.

THREE

An – – – – – came, perhaps, to that Greek shore
Where – – – – – studied medicine apart,
To help him – – – – – the truths from ancient lore
And write, from a new – – – – –, of his art.

FOUR

– – – – – starts the Jewel Song.
A second – – – – –? Oh, how wrong!
– – – – – not that poor, misguided thing,
But those who told her she could sing.

FIVE

The – – – – – – a fat folio fills
With tales – – – – – – and lewd quotations.
These – – – – – – of salacious thrills
Are nude, alas, of illustrations.

76

SIX

She, once a $STARLET$, film-land's queen,
Could $STARTLE$ us like some bright mote.
Now Death eclipses all her sheen
And $RATTLES$ in her lovely throat.

SEVEN

In a $SLUMP$ dozed the medium, muttering low,
"Imps sprout from my flesh! Just feel the $LUMPS$ grow!"
But the psychic researcher was not taken in
By the unripened $PLUMS$ that were taped to her skin.

EIGHT

Upon the $PIER$, the tempting Cockney maid
Her rosy charms, not fully $BLEE$, displayed.
Amid that troop of noisy sea-side vendors,
She seemed a – – – –, fresh from Heaven's splendors.

77

NINE

The poor wretch – – – – the tune all wrong,
And taps with his – – – – – foot the while,
Till – – – – – halts him and his song.
How can the sun look down and smile?

TEN

When an unwelcome – – – – – – – comes to call,
The – – – – – – – of great houses counteract
His – – – – – – – and his overweening gall
With – – – – – – – force, which masquerades as tact.

ELEVEN

Blonde – – – – plans to sell poor fields
And worthless – – – – to clients moneyed.
With – – – – she'll ply each, till he yields,
Then – – – – the – – – – with kisses honeyed.

TWELVE

The learned scholar's voice was gruff.
"You ask what – – – – – means," he said.
"The question's hard, as hard and rough
"As is this – – – – – on which we tread.
"Or, as a man first casts his net,
"Then – – – – – it in despite its weight,
"So is it with this question yet:
"So heavy and so obdurate.
"But Time, that – – – – –, also reveals,
"So you must – – – – – your haste absurd,
"Till scholarship someday unseals
"The meaning of the psalmist's word!"
His pupil said, "Why drone on so,
"If all you mean is 'I don't know'?"

THIRTEEN

This – – – – – paradise invites repose.
The lazy hours – – – – – gently into days.
Yet he who – – – – – long may end like those
Who – – – – – up to beg, and shun our gaze.

FOURTEEN

When tourist – – – – – – – photograph this town,
The ladies – – – – – – – among the young male Turks
And, if they plunk the odd – – – – – – – down,
Get their reward in photogenic smirks.

FIFTEEN

A clumsy hunter may – – – – – – his guides,
Or scold his – – – – – – when the quarry hides,
Demand a – – – – – – on his gun, but still
Cannot conceal his own deficient skill.

SIXTEEN

How _ALIEN_ they were to all she knew—
These _ALIEN_ creatures mumbling in the ward!
Dared she _ALINE_ herself with that small crew
Who helped these helpless, whom the world ignored?

SEVENTEEN

King – – – – loved to hunt and ride,
Or – – – –, on rainy days, inside.
His favorite – – – – ate at his table.
His extra throne was in the stable.

EIGHTEEN

I serve hot – – – – –, while the rich crowds play
Along the – – – – – in sun and surf all day
And, nightly, in fine – – – – – and gowns return,
Each scarf or – – – – – covering a burn.

NINETEEN

The – – – – – – – await their turns to dance and play,
But first this pompous – – – – – – – has his say.
With lordly – – – – – – – and with chest puffed out,
He'd fill our strutting – – – – – – – with self-doubt!

TWENTY

To pay for daily $BREAD$ and weekly rent,
He $BARED$ his body for the world to see.
Though thrilled by $BEARD$ and brawn, his friends who went
$DEBAR$ him now from their society.

A TANGLE OF TWISTERS

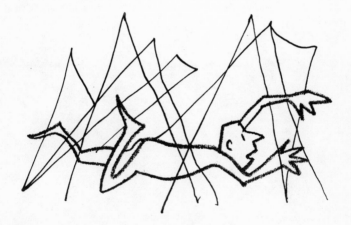

ONE

They peer through _panes_ within the cabin warm,
But shivers creep along their _napes_ and heads.
They see the _aspen_ bow before the storm
And oaks torn, groaning, from their earthy beds.

TWO

Young _Eros_ mainly pleases with his dart,
Although the wound is _sore_ from day to day.
Long-buried _ores_, new-found, gleam in the heart
And love springs like a _rose_ from thawing clay.

THREE

You – – – – –, that with affected manners go,
Break loose the – – – – – of pose and studied art!
Learn Nature's simple grace from streams that flow,
Or from the – – – – – that, budding, moves the heart.

FOUR

To please the S A T Y R dwelling in the wood,
She brought, each evening, T R A Y S of fruit and meat
Which later, found consumed, foretold great good
(Though likely, some poor S T R A Y had wolfed her treat).

FIVE

He sensed a – – – – – fixed on his nape
And, setting down his – – – – –, turned
To face a stuffed but – – – – – ape
Whose – – – – – glass eye upon him burned.

SIX

The two kings sat before the great chess board.
Their prize—poor maiden!—trembling bowed her head.
A final move . . . The bearded ruler roared,
"N O W will you O W N I've W O N her for my bed?"

SEVEN

Very little – – – – – – the Bactrian camel—
Neither – – – – – – monsoon nor market-place trammel.
You can race him for miles, till your bottom is sore,
And when you've scarcely – – – – – –, he's ready for more!

86

THE TWISTERS UNTWISTED

NATURE

1. nets, tens, Sent, nest
2. apes, peas, apse
3. items, mites, smite, times, emits
4. hoes, shoe, hose
5. lows, slow, owls
6. shear, hares, hears, share
7. Late, tale, teal
8. Snug, gnus, guns, sung
9. lame, meal, male
10. teams, meats, steam, Mates, tames
11. limes, miles, slime, limes
12. Scat, cast, cats, acts
13. sepal, pales, lapse, leaps
14. foster, softer, forest
15. tugs, gust, guts
16. Kates, Stake, Keats, Skate, steak, teaks, Takes
17. mane, mean, name, Amen
18. lave, vale, veal
19. gander, Ranged, danger, garden
20. shriek, Hikers, shrike

LOVE GONE SOUR

1. pats, taps, past, spat
2. tales, stale, least, steal
3. raped, drape, padre, pared
4. priest, stripe, sprite, ripest
5. resound, Undoers, sounder
6. ladies, Sailed, aisled, Ideals
7. sang, snag, nags

OUT OF MY WITS TWISTERS

1. plea, peal, pale, leap
2. sliver, silver, livers
3. mar, ram, arm

4. slit, list, silt
5. huts, shut, Tush, Thus
6. cater, react, create, trace
7. tire, tier, rite
8. sloop, pools, loops, spool
9. Ides, side, dies
10. odor, rood, door
11. gores, gorse, ogres
12. spar, Raps, rasp
13. recants, canters, trances
14. slough, loughs, ghouls, slough
15. wines, sinew, swine
16. piecers, recipes, precise, pierces
17. respect, scepter, specter
18. discern, cinders, Rescind
19. layers, relays, slayer
20. slink, kilns, links

HOPES AND THOUGHTS

1. peon, pone, open
2. edit, diet, Tied, tide
3. verse, serve, sever, veers
4. acres, cares, races, scare
5. hardest, threads, hatreds
6. user, ruse, sure, rues
7. arches, chaser, search
8. peaks, spake, Speak
9. lucre, ulcer, cruel
10. Alined, Daniel, nailed, denial
11. eras, ares, ears, sear
12. timer, merit, miter, remit
13. eastern, earnest, nearest
14. occurs, succor, crocus
15. phase, shape, heaps
16. wean, wane, Anew
17. aside, aides, ideas
18. relived, reviled, deliver

19. eluded, delude, dueled
20. phraser, harpers, sharper

FOOD AND DRINK

1. sing, sign, gins
2. bared, beard, bread
3. dame, Edam, mead, made
4. naps, span, pans, snap
5. west, wets, stew
6. Lemnos, solemn, melons, lemons
7. mace, came, acme
8. nuts, tuns, stun
9. tips, Spit, pits
10. gums, smug, Mugs
11. leeks, sleek, keels
12. being, begin, binge
13. rhea, hare, hear
14. cartels, clarets, scarlet
15. recrate, terrace, caterer, retrace

SEA, SKY, AND OPEN SPACES

1. ways, yaws, sway
2. redfin, finder, friend
3. salts, slats, lasts
4. strait, artist, traits
5. revels, elvers, levers
6. emir, rime, mire
7. silent, tinsel, enlist, inlets, listen
8. ropes, prose, spore, pores, Repos
9. paces, space, capes
10. sublet, bustle, bluest, bluets, subtle
11. points, pintos, piston
12. seam, same, mesa
13. ether, three, there
14. cars, arcs, scar
15. tsar, star, rats, arts, tars
16. itself, filets, stifle
17. arise, raise, Aries
18. glisten, tingles, singlet
19. races, acres, scare, cares

20. owns, sown, snow

PIETY AND POSE

1. sober, robes, Bores
2. icons, scion, coins
3. Palms, lamps, psalm
4. prates, paters, repast, Tapers
5. dilatory, adroitly, idolatry
6. wroth, worth, throw
7. agnostic, coasting, coatings
8. shaper, seraph, phrase
9. chaste, sachet, scathe, cheats
10. cadres, cedars, scared, sacred
11. dais, aids, said
12. nave, Evan, vane
13. saint, stain, satin
14. pater, apter, taper, prate
15. aves, save, vase

POLITICS, PRIDE, AND PRICE

1. Heats, hates, haste
2. brag, garb, Grab
3. pines, snipe, spine
4. slave, laves, salve, vales
5. slain, nails, snail
6. shorten, thrones, hornets
7. reveres, reverse, reserve, Severer
8. warder, drawer, warred, reward
9. signet, tinges, ingest
10. news, wens, sewn
11. retails, realist, saltier
12. hatters, shatter, threats
13. hares, hears, share, shear
14. rawest, waters, waster
15. overt, voter, trove
16. critters, restrict, stricter
17. tache, cheat, teach
18. slot, lots, lost
19. sager, gears, rages
20. related, altered, alerted, redealt, treadle

PASTIMES, PEOPLE, AND PROFESSIONS

1. dare, Erda, dear, read
2. tuba, abut, tabu
3. angel, Galen, glean, angle
4. Mabel, Melba, Blame
5. squire, risqué, quires
6. starlet, startle, rattles
7. slump, lumps, plums
8. pier, ripe, peri
9. plays, splay, palsy
10. bustler, butlers, bluster, subtler
11. Elsa, leas, ales, seal, sale
12. selah, shale, hales, heals, leash
13. isled, slide, idles, sidle
14. parties, traipse, piaster
15. berate, beater, rebate
16. alien, anile, aline
17. Olaf, loaf, foal
18. tacos, coast, coats, ascot
19. troupes, spouter, posture, pouters
20. bread, bared, beard, Debar

A TANGLE OF TWISTERS

1. panes, napes, aspen
2. Eros, sore, ores, rose
3. prigs, grips, sprig
4. satyr, trays, stray
5. glare, lager, regal, large
6. Now, own, won
7. deters, desert, rested